Seasons
of the Year

Las estaciones
del año

Winter/
Invierno

by/por JoAnn Early Macken

Reading consultant/Consultora de lectura:
Susan Nations, M.Ed.,
author, literacy coach,
and consultant in literacy development/
autora, tutora de alfabetización,
y consultora de desarrollo de la lectura

Please visit our web site at: www.garethstevens.com
For a free color catalog describing Weekly Reader® Early Learning Library's list
of high-quality books, call 1-877-445-5824.

Library of Congress Cataloging-in-Publication Data

Macken, JoAnn Early, 1953-
   [Winter. Spanish & English]
   Winter = Invierno / by JoAnn Early Macken.
      p. cm. — (Seasons of the year = Las estaciones del año)
   title: Invierno.
   ISBN-10: 0-8368-6535-6 (lib. bdg.)
   ISBN-13: 978-0-8368-6535-9 (lib. bdg.)
   ISBN-10: 0-8368-6540-5 (softcover)
   ISBN-13: 978-0-8368-6540-0 (softcover)
   1. Winter—Juvenile literature. I. Title: Invierno. II. Title.
  QB637.8.M3318   2006
  508.2—dc22   2005030510

This edition first published in 2006 by
Weekly Reader Books
An imprint of Gareth Stevens Publishing
200 First Stamford Place
Stamford, CT 06912 USA

Copyright © 2006 by Weekly Reader® Early Learning Library

Art direction: Tammy West
Cover design and page layout: Kami Strunsee
Translators: Tatiana Acosta and Guillermo Gutiérrez
Picture research: Cisley Celmer

Photo credits: Cover, p. 10 © Barbara Stitzer/PhotoEdit; p. 4 © Mary Steinbacher/
PhotoEdit; pp. 5, 8, 9 © Gibson Stock Photography; p. 6 © Robert Brenner/PhotoEdit;
p. 7 © Cathy Melloan Resources/PhotoEdit; p. 11 © The Image Bank/Getty Images;
pp. 12, 14 © Lon C. Diehl/PhotoEdit; p. 13 © Seymour Hewitt/Ionica/Getty Images;
p. 15 © Richard Hutchings/Photo Researchers, Inc.; p. 16 (all) © Hemera

Printed in the United States of America

2 3 4 5 6 7 8 9 10 09 08 07

Note to Educators and Parents

Learning to read is one of the most exciting and challenging things young children do. Among other skills, they are beginning to match the spoken word to print and learn directionality and print conventions. Books that are appropriate for emergent readers will incorporate many of these conventions while also being appealing and entertaining.

The books in the *Seasons of the Year* series are designed to support young readers in the earliest stages of literacy. They will love looking at the full color photographs while learning about the exciting world of seasonal changes and differences. Each book will invite children to read—and reread—again and again!

In addition to serving as wonderful picture books in schools, libraries, and homes, this series is specifically intended to be read within instructional small groups. The small group setting enables the teacher or other adult to provide scaffolding that will boost the reader's efforts. Children and adults alike will find these books supportive, engaging, and fun!

— Susan Nations, M.Ed., author, literacy coach,
and consultant in literacy development

Nota para los maestros y los padres

Aprender a leer es una de las actividades más emocionantes y estimulantes para los niños pequeños. Entre otras destrezas, los niños están comenzando a entender la relación entre el lenguaje oral y el escrito, y a aprender convenciones de la letra impresa como la dirección de lectura. Los libros apropiados para lectores incipientes deben incorporar muchas de estas convenciones, además de resultar atrayentes e interesantes.

Los libros de la colección *Las estaciones del año* están pensados para apoyar a los jóvenes lectores en las primeras etapas de ese aprendizaje. Los niños disfrutarán mirando las fotografías a todo color mientras se introducen en el fascinante mundo de los cambios y diferencias estacionales. ¡Cada libro invitará a los niños a leer — y releer — una y otra vez!

Además de servir como maravillosos libros ilustrados en escuelas, bibliotecas y hogares, estos libros han sido especialmente concebidos para ser leídos en pequeños grupos de lectura guiada. El contexto de un grupo reducido permite que el maestro u otro adulto proporcione el andamiaje en el que se basarán los progresos del lector. ¡Estos libros les resultarán útiles, estimulantes y divertidos a niños y a adultos por igual!

— Susan Nations, M.Ed., autora, tutora de alfabetización,
y consultora de desarrollo de la lectura

Winter is cold.

El invierno es frío.

Snow falls.

———

Cae la nieve.

We catch it.

La agarramos.

We shovel it.
_____
La paleamos.

We ski.

———

Esquiamos.

We ride.

———————

Vamos en trineo.

We skate.

———————

Patinamos.

We slide.

———

Nos deslizamos.

We pat.

———————

Damos golpecitos.

We roll.

———

Formamos bolas.

We build
_____

¡Hacemos

a snowman!

———————

un muñeco de nieve!

Glossary/Glosario

shovel/pala

ski/esquiar

skate/patín

**snowman/
muñeco de nieve**